Yours, Mine & God's

Other books written by
Michelle Whitaker Winfrey

It's My Birthday... Finally! A Leap Year Story

It's My Birthday... Finally! A Leap Year Story Activity Book

Yours, Mine & God's
Giving and Receiving
All for the Love of
God
and the Church

Michelle Whitaker Winfrey

Copyright © 2005 by Michelle Whitaker Winfrey

All rights reserved, including the right to reproduce this book or any part thereof in any form, except for inclusion of brief excerpts used in published reviews, without written permission.

Hobby House Publishing Group
P.O. Box 1527
Jackson, NJ 08527

www.hobbyhousepublishinggroup.com

ISBN 10: 0-9727179-3-5
ISBN 13: 978-0-9727179-3-9
Library of Congress Control Number: 2005932636

Frog carrying mushroom with or without the double H is a Trademark of Hobby House Publishing Group

Unless otherwise noted, all scripture references are taken from the King James Version found at www.Godrules.net. Used with permission.

Printed in the United States of America

This book is dedicated to the
Liturgical Dancers of Living Word Christian Fellowship
Neptune, New Jersey, USA
"Spirit and Truth"

I thank this wonderfully diverse and talented group
of women and one man for their time, energy and love for God.
Dancing with them completed a part of my journey,
and allowed the word of God to enter my soul
and pour onto paper – hence this book.

"What a blessing it is to DANCE for the Lord"

ಸಾ

To my mom, for without her commitment to God my relationship
with the Lord may not have deepened.

Special Thanks
to those who granted me permission to
use their words in making this book come to life!

(Listed in order of quote appearance)

Father Francis N. Hebert
Dr. Rick L. Patterson
Will Vanderburg
The Reverend Cedric A. Miller
The Barna Group
The Reverend Linda Hunt
Mark Willis

Edited by Jeannette Cézanne
Customline Wordware, Inc.
www.customline.com

Contents

List of Charts, Forms and Exercises – Page ix

List of Bible Verses – Page xi

Foreword – The Reverend Cedric A. Miller – Page xiii

Acknowledgements – Page xvi

Introduction – Page 17

Chapter 1 How to Use this Book – Page 25
- Workbook, Guide and Information
- Taking Notes

Chapter 2 The Mission Statement – Page 33
- For the Church
- For the Congregation… for You!

Chapter 3 Understanding Giving – Page 39
- Americans Donate Billions to Charity
- For the Congregation …for You!
  Why Do You Make Your Current Giving Decisions?
- For the Church:
  Why Do You Think Your Congregation Makes the Giving Decisions it Makes?

Chapter 4 What do You Have to Give? – Page 53
- Money, Time, Talent and Skills, In-Kind Services and Donations
- Principle of Divine Ownership vs. the Principle of Dominion
- 10 Ways for You to Give to Your Church

Chapter 5 Understanding Your Personal Financial Situation – Page 71
- What is Your Current Level of Giving to the Church?
- Understanding Your Personal Budget

Chapter 6 Understanding the Needs of the Church – Page 81
- How Well do You Know Your Church?

Chapter 7 Let the Church Speak – Page 87
- Annual Report
- Financial Profile
- Profile of Activities and Ministries
- Fun, Fun, Fun and Fundraising

Chapter 8 Getting the Word Out – Page 103
- Communications

Chapter 9 A Sure Negative Response – Page 111
- 10 Things Not to do When Asking for Time and/or Money

Chapter 10 How to Receive More – Page 117
- 10 Ways to Assist Your Congregation in Giving More

Chapter 11 A Word to the Faithful – Page 127
- Discern, Disclose and Deliver

About the Author – Page 135

"And whatsoever ye do, do it heartily, as to the Lord, and not unto men"
Colossians 3:23

List of Charts, Forms and Exercises

For the Congregation... for You!   **Page**

- Personal Mission Statement   36
- Mission Statement of Your Church   37
- How Your Giving Decisions Are Made   49
- Giving Profile   73
- Personal Income Worksheet   77
- Personal Expense Worksheet   78
- Monthly Expense Tracking Worksheet   79
- Giving Chart   83
- Questionnaire: How Well Do You Know
  Your Church   84

For the Church

- Church Mission Statement   34
- Why Giving Decisions are Made   51
- Annual Report Statistics Worksheet   90
- Financial Profile Income Worksheet   92
- Financial Profile Expense Worksheet   93
- Activities and Ministries Awareness
  Worksheet   96
- Ministry and Program Closure Report   97
- Profile of Church Communications   104
- Family/Household Profile Form   124
- Change of Information Form   125

List of Bible Verses

	Page
• Colossians 3:23	viii
• Leviticus 27:30	17
• Leviticus 27:32	17
• Romans 14:8	37
• Acts 2:46	38
• Deuteronomy 14:22	55
• Genesis 1:28	57
• Malachi 3:10	59
• Proverbs 3:9	60
• Exodus 35:29	63
• Acts 20:35	76
• Acts 2:44	77
• Deuteronomy 16:17	80
• Exodus 25:21	84
• Psalms 24:1	85
• Exodus 25:2	89
• Luke 6:38	100
• Romans 12:2	101
• Numbers 18:21	103
• Luke 4:4	111
• Deuteronomy 14:28	117
• Deuteronomy 14:29	121

Foreword
The Reverend Cedric A. Miller

Nineteen years ago I embarked upon this journey of the pastorate. Filled with zeal, charisma, and a confident knowing that the Lord had indeed called me to plant a church, I was fearless in this endeavor. I was armed with only a secular education, and a lifetime of classical Pentecostalism centered mostly around small churches that were attended by other lifers of the same tradition.

Growing up, stewardship was never mentioned much. I cannot imagine anyone in my father's church not tithing. After all, tithers stood in the center aisle for all to see and non-tithers would be confronted by the eldership and appropriately reprimanded or punished. In fact you couldn't participate in ministry without being a tither. Services offered by the church were available only to tithers. There was no mistaking it, stewardship, and tithing in particular was synonymous with salvation. Everyone knew that if you loved the Lord, you showed it by tithing and otherwise supporting the church and the work of the Lord. Church clean up days garnered attendances that rivaled a regular church service. No one except for the pastor and maybe a part-time clerical worker was compensated. Who would dare charge to work for the Lord? The very thought of needing a strategy to encourage Christians to give to God's work would have been looked upon with incredulity.

Then there was the idea of the official church board. I hope by now you are laughing with me and not at me. Church boards were for those non-spirit-filled churches that did not believe in the gifts of the spirit and accordingly did not have a leader who could hear from the Lord and get direction for the congregation. No one dared question the authority, integrity or wisdom of the pastor. To inquire or even express a faint curiosity in the financial dealings of the church would be considered, immature, disloyal, suspicious of leadership and out of order. Pastors answered only to God and you didn't question/touch the Lord's anointed.

Does this sound like a foreign land, far away from here? Well, it was and someone forgot to inform me that the times and people had changed. Churches now have tax exempt status that come with certain requirements. I was too young to know at the time, but that old system, though noble and had some semblances of biblical truths, experienced a lot of abuse, mismanagement, poor decision making and down right fraud.

No wonder so many chickens gave their lives for the sake of the gospel. Church members were not educated in the area of personal finances. Churches were ignorant as to the need for: timely and relevant information of, church finances, ministry opportunities, services offered, the needs of the church, a system of accountability of church leaders, frequent encouragement and involvement in financial matters, and a solid and continuous teaching about what the bible has to say about our attitude and responsibility regarding money, in and out of the church.

Had someone placed such a foundational though thorough work as *Yours, Mine and God's* in my hands nineteen years ago, I could have avoided a lot of pitfalls and mistakes over the years. I watched good people leave the ministry because I did not understand their needs or the post-modern attitude toward the church and its financial dealings. Many I might have thought of as uncommitted may have just needed help with their personal finances, a better understanding of scripture, or simply some encouragement and information from their pastor.

My enthusiastic recommendation of this book is twofold. First, it is my sincerest desire that no other pastor enter into ministry as unprepared as I was in this area and consequently make the same mistakes that I did. Secondly, that member of the body of Christ would take personal responsibility to educate themselves about the finances, services, ministry opportunities, financial and human needs, and biblical responsibility to their local church.

This book is recommended for; new pastors, ill-prepared pastors, new convert or foundation course teachers and everyone wishing to improve their serve to their local church in the area of stewardship and overall involvement. It may be cliché but if I knew then what I know now, I could have avoided many heartaches and undoubtedly be further along in ministry.

Acknowledgements

I would like to thank ...

The Reverend Cedric A. Miller for his gift of deliverance
and powerful beliefs.
When I met him my faith was in a quandary,
I graciously thank him for helping me find my way.
(Senior Pastor, Living Word Christian Fellowship, Neptune, NJ)

The Honorable James D. Manning for speaking the truth.
"Her faith is within."
(Reverend, Atlah World Ministries, Atlah, NY)

Father Francis N. Hebert for asking me to sit on the vestry.
This mission was the spark for writing this book.
(Rector, St. Peter's Episcopal Church, Freehold, NJ)

Mother Idalia Craig for being there,
and knowing she will always be there.

Introduction

I have been an Episcopalian most of my life. Growing up in a home where my father was an Episcopalian and my mother a Baptist, I learned to understand and appreciate both Protestant denominations.

In writing this book, I do not profess to be a theological scholar. I am a Christian who has questioned my own giving practices. As a member of the congregation, I listened and saw the reactions of the congregation around me when the subject of stewardship was discussed. I challenged these reactions against my own. As a member of the congregation, it was never enough for me to simply be told that the budget is short… I needed to know why, how and by how much.

> *"And all the tithe of the land, whether of the seed of the land,*
> *or of the fruit of the tree, is the Lord's:*
> *it is holy unto the Lord."*
> Leviticus 27:30

> *"And concerning the tithe of the herd, or of the flock,*
> *even of whatsoever passeth under the rod,*
> *the tenth shall be holy unto the Lord."*
> Leviticus 27:32

Why do we read the Bible, understand the Bible, and even agree with the Bible, yet do not give our blessings proportionally to the church?

Somehow, we fail to see that money, time and talent are needed in order to keep the church operational. Is that because we do not see the church as a viable not-for-profit business entity that has expenses and needs, in the way we may view a theater company?

This book was written to help ministers, lay ministers and stewardship leaders in leading their congregations to greater giving; and for the people of the congregation who are struggling to gain a better understanding of *giving* to the church.

In Genesis there are clear indications of what God wants from us. As we progress through this book we will focus on the following:

Stewardship
Giving of Gifts
Receiving of Gifts

The purpose of this book is twofold:

1. This book is not to tell you what you should or should not do, but rather to get you to think about what you are presently doing. It is a tool that can be followed in whole, or in part, to suit your needs and those of the church and the congregation.

2. This book is not to tell you that you must tithe, but rather to educate you on why you should financially support and be involved with your church. It is to help you establish a healthy and comfortable level of giving and support. And it is to assist the church in developing different approaches to increase giving and the development of gracious receiving.

Throughout this book there are useful charts, forms and exercises that can be done individually or in groups. These exercises are designed to assist you in evaluating your church as well as yourself. Some exercises may help clarify many aspects of your church life as well as your personal life.

As you progress through this book, remember that everything you have is a gift from God.

> "Stewardship is about what we do in every area of our lives. It is about making an intentional determination about how we will spend the wealth of time, talent and treasure that God has entrusted to us."
>
> Father Francis N. Hebert
> St. Peter's Episcopal Church
> Freehold, New Jersey
> The Peppercorn, October 2005

I did not always understand or believe the writings within these pages. It was not until after many years of sitting on the vestry and the Long-Range Planning Strategic Committee, after hosting cottage meetings and chairing various other events and ministries within the church that I discovered that I was not giving enough. Mind you, I always pledged. It was during an 18-month sojourn when I reevaluated several aspects of my life (spiritually, mentally, physically and financially) that the revelation to write this book came to me. Even then, I could not write it. I was not ready until God said I was. Having made notes for this book over the 18 months I was finally able to sit down and begin writing on April 11, 2005. I began tithing in January of that year.

> One day I was talking to a friend about this book and giving to the church. During the conversation she admitted that she did not give proportionately to her church. I asked her why. Her response was that she was insulted that the "church" should tell her how much she should give. I then asked her if she knew how much it

cost to operate her church. She did not know. I asked her if she felt fulfilled when leaving church and if her $10 was an equal match to her fulfillment. She looked at me stunned and replied, "no, absolutely not." She had not matched her giving with what she was receiving. In addition, she had not accounted for all the services provided by the church because, at this time, she did not use or need many of them.

So many of us fall into this category, into this type of thinking.

If this book opens the mind of one person and gets him or her to give more and assist one church in leading their congregation to giving more, then the book's purpose has been fulfilled. I believe that God placed me on the path to write this book not because the writing of this book will cause me to increase my giving… I have already done that.

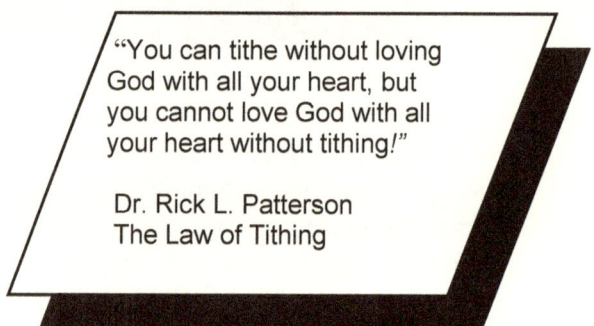

"You can tithe without loving God with all your heart, but you cannot love God with all your heart without tithing!"

Dr. Rick L. Patterson
The Law of Tithing

Do you love the Lord?

Listen to His teachings, listen to the teachings of your pastor, and look at your life as it is today. Close your eyes and see your life as you would like it to be. Marvel at the bounty of your blessings. How many televisions do you have? Do your children get new shoes every year for school? What are your talents? How blessed are you?

There are Seven Wonders of the World, but only one wonder that is out of this world: GOD!

An outpouring of my soul developed this book. My love for God and complete awe of His powers are within these pages. Take all you need from this book and use it to build your church and to build yourself. Grow in knowledge and understanding and say "hallelujah" as you share your growth with your family, friends, pastor and fellow parishioners.

Lead your congregation to giving more.

> *Remember the old joke about the scientist who challenged God and said, "I've discovered the secret! I, a mere human being can create life!" "Okay,' says God, "show me." The scientist begins by saying, "first I'll need some dirt..."*
>
> *God's reply? "Make your own dirt!"*[1]

---

[1] The Peppercorn, October 2005, St. Peter's Episcopal Church, Freehold, New Jersey, Father Francis N. Hebert.

Yours, Mine & God's

Yours, Mine & God's
Giving and Receiving
All for the Love of God
and the Church

The church is a self-supporting organization that relies on the gifts, time and talents of its members to stay alive!

Will Vanderburg

Chapter 1
How to Use this Book

Workbook, Guide and Information

The Bible teaches us that giving is a gracious act of obedience. The attitude we have toward giving carries over into how we worship. If we live as gracious worshipers, and tithe per God's Word, we will live a blessed life.

If you are a pastor, this book is to get you to look at yourself, and your church, its leaders and congregation, so that you can incite increased giving. If you are a parishioner, this book will help you look at yourself and your church, its leaders and ministries, and offer you ways to increase your giving. If you are not willing to try new things, this book is not for you.

Dr. Rick L. Patterson, Th.D., President, Miami Christian University wrote a paper titled "The Law of Tithing." [2] In this paper he writes about Christian maturity and the attitude that extends from this growth.

---

[2] Dr. Rick L. Patterson, ThD., President, Miami Christian University, 9775 SW 87 Avenue, Miami, Florida 33176 – www.mcu.edu & www.patterson.org. "The Law of Tithing."

> "Christian maturity is not being based upon the concept of 'God, what can you give me?' Rather, it is an attitude which expresses gratitude to God, and a thank you, Lord, for what you have done for me, now what can I do for you in return? Mature Christians see the need and fill it. They see their responsibility and respond to it."

There are two ways to use this book. Select the way that best suits your needs.

1. You may choose to read this book from cover to cover.

2. You may select specific chapters and sections that are of interest to you.

There are various exercises throughout the book. When doing the exercises, you should be as honest as possible. When you are unsure of an answer, indicate that in your notes, and return to it later.

Church leaders should do the exercises individually. One person should analyze the results and share them with the group. It is recommended that a discussion follow in order to determine how people arrived at their answers and where the group is divided. Division among leadership in any organization is not healthy for growth and stability.

Although this book is interspersed with separate sections for the clergy and the congregation, it is highly recommended that both groups read the entire book. It was not until I learned what went on "behind the scenes" by sitting on the vestry and other committees that I understood what it cost to operate a church, as well as gaining a greater understanding and respect for how the church functions. If you are not involved, you may only see your pastor two to three hours a week on Sunday morning. I have learned that this is an unrealistic presentation of the job at hand. Many pastors are on call and work six and seven days a week, including holidays!

At some point in his or her life, each pastor was not a pastor, but rather a member of the congregation. This book will help them to go back to that time and recall how they felt about giving prior to gaining their present level of understanding.

This book is also written for the parishioner who wants to give and/or increase his or her current level of giving, as well as for the church that is open to new thoughts and ideas on how to increase giving. A partnership between the two is then developed.

For the Church

"We never seem to have enough money!"

"The summer months are always tough."

"Based on the amount collected each Sunday, the median income of each family is approximately $10,000 a year. Is that possible?"

"For the past four weeks we had to ask for money just to get through."

If you have ever made any of these remarks, this book is for you and your church leaders!

Although this book is about giving – tithing – it does not discuss tithing from a theological perspective... I am leaving that up to you. In order to keep your spirit in tune with what the Bible says, we have placed scripture quotations throughout this book.

Yours, Mine & God's is designed to help you better communicate with your associate pastors, lay ministers and congregation. When you complete this book and the exercises in it, you will hopefully be able to lead your church to greater giving.

Not every exercise and suggestion will be for you and your church. Pick and choose what you believe will work for your situation. There is too much information in this book to try to implement all at once. Take your time, consider your options, develop a prayerful plan and watch yourself and your church grow!

How to Use this Book

For the Congregation... for You!

"I can't afford to give more!"

"Why should I give more?"

"Where is my money going?"

"I find it insulting that someone is telling me how much to give!"

"It's my money; I'll donate what I want, to whom I want!"

If you have ever expressed any of these sentiments, this book is for you.

Although this book makes constant reference to "tithing," we do recommend that you seek guidance from your pastor and church leaders for a greater spiritual and theological understanding of tithing.

Yours, Mine & God's is designed to help you determine your giving level and reach the goal of tithing (giving 10%) or more of your income to the church. The exercises in this book may be repeated over the course of several years as your financial situation changes and your spirituality matures.

There are different schools of thought regarding tithing as to whether it should be before or after tax. Although we do not make a decision for you in this book, we will address it briefly when we address the subject of budgeting. Please discuss this with your pastor if you are in need of guidance.

Regardless of whether you choose to give before or after tax, you should remember one simple rule:

Yours, Mine & God's

Pay God first and have faith that God's return will be great!

*Remember that God's return is not necessarily in money.
It can also be in the form of a new job, a home or car.
It can even be a blessing upon your children.*

"Faith requires <u>action</u>."

The Reverend Cedric A. Miller
Living Word Christian Fellowship
Neptune, New Jersey

How to Use this Book

For the Church & Congregation

Taking notes

The process of writing notes and messages is critical to your success in using this book. In order to help you to remember to write notes, and to provide you with a place to write these notes, we have inserted note sections throughout the study.

Look for this symbol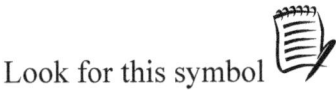

Writing notes will help you understand your personal growth and the growth of your congregation and church. Make it a point to read your notes periodically. As you progress through the book it is hoped that your thoughts and understanding about giving will change, grow and mature.

10% (the tithe) is used as the base level of giving in this book.

<u>Special Note</u>

Within this book we make reference to the D'Mode family and their church, *the Giving Church*. Please note that Mr. and Mrs. William D'Mode (Sally and Bill), along with their three children, David, Anthony and Karen, as well as *the Giving Church* are fictitious, developed for the sole purpose of demonstrating points and examples within this book.

Any similarity to persons living or deceased is purely coincidental.

Yours, Mine & God's

Chapter 2
The Mission Statement

For the Church

Your congregation – current members and new ones – want to know your purpose. A mission statement is one way to communicate it.

Having a mission statement is a fundamental aspect of your church. How can you be sure that your leaders are all on the same path? Continuity is critical to the success of any organization. Within a church, each activity, each lesson, each sermon must flow from the same source. That source is your mission.

If your church has a mission statement, write it in the space provided. Is your mission statement posted in your church or in your weekly bulletin? Is it on your Web site? If the answer to these questions is no, how do you communicate your mission statement to your congregation?

If your church does not have a mission statement, develop one. Do not forget to distribute it to your parishioners.

Here are a few things to think about when developing your mission statement:

1. Make sure your mission statement represents your church as you want it to be seen by the Christian public, reflecting your growth and stability over the years.

2. Your mission statement should be powerful, representing the soul and rhythm of your congregation and its leaders. The mission statement is the heartbeat of your church.

3. Take your time in developing the mission statement of your church. As your church grows in clarity, giving and receiving, be willing to modify the mission statement in order to reflect where your church is at that point in time.

Church Mission Statement   **Date:**

_____

_____

_____

_____

_____

_____

_____

_____

_____

_____

_____

_____

_____

The Mission Statement

For the Congregation... for You!

If you pay God last, you will find that you may be cutting yourself short!

Ask yourself the following questions:

What do you pay God with?
Why do you go to church?
Why do you go to the church you go to?

Whether you are happy in your current church or are looking for a new church, one of the most important things you should read is the church's mission statement. Why does it exist? What is its purpose? Does it meet your needs?

In order to be able to answer any of the above questions, you must first know what you are looking for, and why you are looking for it. Developing a *personal* mission statement is one way to ensure that you are in the right church or that a potential new one is a good match for you.

Think about the following and record your answers:

- Why do you attend your current church?

_____
_____
_____

- What size church are you comfortable in?

_____
_____
_____

- What type of leadership are you looking for?

_____
_____
_____

- Are there specific ministries that you are looking for?

_____
_____
_____

- What type of congregation are you looking for?

_____
_____
_____

Now, write your own mission statement. As you grow, do not be afraid to modify your mission statement.

Personal Mission Statement　　　　　**Date:**

_____
_____
_____
_____
_____
_____

Your mission statement should help keep you on track throughout this book. Make sure that you are, at all times, on the course set forth by your mission statement. This does not mean that you cannot modify your personal mission statement as you grow! Be open to doing this. Modifying your mission statement does not mean that you are unfaithful; it means that you are learning and developing… maturing.

> **Romans 14:8**
> For whether we live, we live unto the Lord; and whether we die, we die unto the Lord: whether we live therefore, or die, we are the Lord's.

What is the mission statement of the church you attend?

The reason you are writing it here is so that you can have easy access to it and compare it to your personal mission statement. If you do not already have a copy of your church's mission statement, ask for it. If your church has a Web site, its mission statement should be available there.

Mission Statement of Your Church

_____
_____
_____
_____
_____
_____
_____
_____
_____

Review the two mission statements. Do your spiritual needs

match what your church has to offer? As you progress through this book, you may need to re-read both mission statements from time to time.

Quite often, as I encounter other Christians in my travels, they ask me, "Where is your church home?" Your church, like your home, has to fit you, your personality; it has to feel comfortable and purposeful. You need to be able to leave your guard at the door and worship openly and freely.

Your church's mission statement can help you determine if you are in the right church – or just going to the nearest church because it is convenient. Convenience is great when it comes to needing milk and eggs; but selecting your church should not be based upon convenience. It should be based upon your thirst; your spiritual needs, and the quenching of that thirst.

The church you choose should bring you closer to God. Are you growing in Christ? Are you encountering the Holy Spirit?

> **Acts 2:46**
> And they, continuing daily with one accord in the temple, and breaking bread from house to house, did eat meat with gladness and singleness of heart.

Are you worshipping God with a fulfilled heart? If you answered no to any of these questions, you may not be going to the right church. If you choose to look for a new church, take your time. When making any major life-altering decision, such as buying a new house, you do not purchase the first home you see!

It is vital to your religious growth that you attend church… not just *any* church, but a church that fits your needs, so you can worship with and among other Christians.

Chapter 3
Understanding Giving

For the Church & Congregation

This chapter focuses on giving practices in the United States. The information here will help you determine where you are in your giving practices. It will also help you understand and determine if what you are presently giving is enough. Do you believe that what you are currently giving to your church is a sufficient amount for what you are receiving?

Remember this as you read this chapter: If you were in the hospital, in need of prayer or spiritual guidance, who would you call? When it is time for your wedding or the wedding of your children, where will it take place? Who do you want to officiate at your funeral? Who teaches Sunday school, and where do the materials come from? Each month you receive a newsletter or calendar; who pays for it, types, prints, and distributes it? When you call the church office, is someone there to answer the phone? Is the church warm in the winter? Everything mentioned here has a cost, a value, either monetary or measured in time.

How much did you give last Sunday? Is this enough to cover all the services and benefits you receive?

What about the pastor? Do you believe in, support and thank your pastor? What do you give back to your pastor? Did the sermon reach you? Did he or she lead you closer to Christ? Do the words your pastor speaks offer you solace and guidance? Did you leave the church with a greater sense of fulfillment than when you arrived? Are you well-fed and ready to take on the week's activities? If you answered yes to any of these questions, do you thank your pastor? Or do you take the outpouring of that person's wisdom and knowledge for granted?

What would happen if you went to church and there was no preacher? How would the Word of God be fed to you? Someone would eventually take over and preach the Word of God. Why? Because, as children of God, we yearn to hear God's Word. The Bible tells us that we need to attend church and be in the presence of other Christians. This is critical to our growth and continued maturity. As Christian and as committed as you can be, you cannot receive fulfillment at home alone. The leader of your community of faith is critical to your growth. In determining your giving level, remember to include your pastor.

How much did you give last Sunday? Was it enough?

Look at the amount you leave in the plate or basket each Sunday, and determine its value. Is $10 or $20 enough to cover all that you receive from your church? You probably spend more than that on a movie and popcorn! Did that movie take you closer to Christ? Will you call upon the producers of that movie when you are in a crisis or in need of prayer?

If your church has 300 adults, and each gave $20 weekly for 52 weeks, your church's income would be $390,000 annually. However, this is not a realistic number. 300 adults may equate to approximately 200 families or 500 members when you add in children and other dependents, which drastically reduces the overall impact. Many families give as one unit, not as individual adults and children. In many cases, one of the adults – the one

Understanding Giving

who handles the finances – makes the offering. The wedding band signifies that the married couple and/or family constitutes one unit, yes: however, within the church, you benefit not only as a family, but each person benefits as an individual as well.

Example:

Before you got married, you were giving $25.00 per week to the church. After you married, you and your husband began attending church together. Did you increase your giving to $50.00 per week in order to account for both of you, or are you still giving $25.00?

Many couples decide to keep their tithes separate. Either way is fine. Just take a moment to look at how you and your spouse are giving.

When you had a child, did you increase your giving? Remember, our children also receive blessings from the Lord.

Americans Donate Billions to Charity, But Giving to Churches Has Declined[3]

Research shows that Americans give away enormous sums of money every year. In April 2005, the Barna Group published its annual survey of religious behavior. This report shows that in 2004, Americans continued their previous pattern of giving to not-for-profit organizations and churches. Although significant in numbers, the overall dollar amount is not increasing.

A Large Majority Gives Away Money
In 2004, nearly four out of every five adults – 83% – donated money to one or more not-for-profit organizations. That is similar to the percentage that has donated funds throughout the past decade. Barna's national study found that the people least likely to donate any money at all were those under the age of 25, people who never attended college, residents of the northeast, atheists and agnostics, and Asians and Hispanics. A quarter or more of the people from each of those segments failed to give away any money in 2004.

The average amount of money donated per person was $1232. That suggests that the typical individual gave away about 3% of his or her income.

---

[3] The statistics used in this chapter are taken from the published survey results of the Barna Group. The Barna Group, Ltd., and its research division (the Barna Research Group), is a privately held, for-profit corporation that conducts primary research, produces visual media and books, and facilitates the healthy development of leaders, children, families and Christian ministries. Located in Ventura, California, Barna has been conducting and analyzing primary research to understand cultural trends related to values, beliefs, attitudes and behaviors since 1984. If you would like to receive free email notification of the release of each new bi-weekly update on the latest research findings from the Barna Group, you may subscribe to this free service at the Barna Web site at www.barna.org.

Church Donations Are Substantial
Churches receive the largest share of the money donated each year. In 2004, two-thirds of all adults (65%) donated some money to a church or other place of worship.

The people most likely to have given money to a religious center in the past year were Protestants (76%), upscale adults (77%), political conservatives (80%), born-again Christians (85%), and evangelical Christians (97%).

The average amount of money donated to churches was $895 per donor in 2004. On the face of it, that sum appears healthy: it is substantially more than the average amounts over each of the past several years. However, when inflation is factored in, the current dollar average is actually less than the amount that houses of worship received in the late 1990s. From 1999 through 2004, cumulative annual giving to churches increased by $89 per donor, representing an 11% rise since before the turn of the millennium. After factoring in inflation, however, churches are actually getting about 2% less than the current value of the money contributed in 1999.

Protestants continue to give more generously to their churches than do Catholics. Protestant adults gave an average of $1304 to churches in 2004, compared to $547 given by the typical Catholic. The most generous donors of all, however, were evangelicals, who averaged $3250 in church giving.

Tithing Is Uncommon
For a number of years, the Barna Group has also been following the practice of "tithing," that is, donating at least ten percent of one's income. While some dispute whether tithing refers to giving the entire ten percent to churches or whether that sum may include money donated to churches and other not-for-profit entities, the survey data reveal that no matter how it is defined, very few Americans tithed in 2004. Only 4% gave such an

amount to churches alone; just 6% gave to either churches or to a combination of churches and para-church ministries.

Although generosity, stewardship and tithing are higher profile issues among born-again Christians than for other people, relatively few born-again adults – only 9% – tithed to churches in 2004. That behavior was most common among evangelicals (23%), and much smaller among non-evangelical born-again Christians (7%), notional Christians (less than 1%), people of other faiths (1%) and atheists and agnostics (none). Overall, 7% of Protestants tithed to churches – divided into 5% among people associated with mainline churches and 8% of those affiliated with other Protestant congregations. Tracking data show that tithing among all born-again adults (i.e., evangelical and non-evangelical, combined) has stayed within a range of 6% to 14% throughout the past decade, varying by a few percentage points since 1999.

Several groups stand out as being particularly tightfisted when it comes to supporting churches financially. Less than 2% of adults under the age of 40, Catholics, and Asians tithed in 2004. A different way of considering "tithing" is by measuring whether the individual donated at least one-tenth of his or her income to not-for-profit organizations, including but not limited to churches and other houses of worship. If the data are evaluated from that vantage point, the percentage of adults who tithe is 6%. Again, the most prolific givers are those whose contributions flow primarily to churches. More than one-quarter of evangelicals (27%) fit this criteria for tithing, compared to 10% among non-evangelical born-again Christians, 1% of notional Christians, 2% of adults aligned with non-Christian faith groups, and 3% of atheists and agnostics.

Why People Do Not Give More
Related studies by the Barna Group offer additional insights into why Americans do not give more money to churches. "There are

five significant barriers to more generous giving," notes George Barna, the study's director.

1. Some people lack the motivation to give away their hard-earned money because the church has failed to provide a compelling vision of how the money will make a difference in the world. These are donors who can find other uses for their money and are not excited about simply handing money over to a church.

2. Those who see their giving as leverage on the future. They withhold money from the church because they do not see a sufficient return on their investment.

3. The third segment is comprised of people who do not realize the church needs their money to be effective. Their church has done an inadequate job of asking for money, so people remain oblivious to the church's expectations and potential.

4. Those who are ignorant of what the Bible teaches about our responsibility to apply God's resources in ways that affect lives.

5. Those who are just selfish. They figure they worked hard for their money and it is theirs to use as they please. Their priorities revolve around their personal needs and desires.

Barna indicates that people often fit into two or more of those categories, making it even more challenging for churches to encourage generosity. "It helps when church leaders recognize the underlying issue related to each of these barriers," the best-selling author continues. "The absence of a compelling vision to motivate generosity is a leadership issue. The perception that donations do not produce significant outcomes is usually an efficiency or productivity issue, sometimes compounded by poor communications. Churches that struggle because they do not ask strategically have a process issue. When the problem is people's ignorance of scriptural principles regarding stewardship, there is a theological or educational issue. And cases where people focus on themselves rather than other people reflect a heart issue. The reality is that Americans are willing to give more generously than they typically do, but it takes a purposeful and well-executed approach to facilitate that generosity."

Research Source and Methodology

The data reported in this summary are based on telephone interviews with a nationwide random sample of 1003 adults conducted in late January of 2005 by the Barna Group. The maximum margin of sampling error associated with the aggregate sample is ±3.2 percentage points at the 95% confidence level. Similar surveys have been conducted every January since 1991 by the company, with random samples of adults, ranging from 1001 to 1205 people. All non-institutionalized adults in the 48 contiguous states were eligible to be interviewed and the distribution of respondents in the survey sample corresponds to the geographic dispersion of the U.S. adult population. The data were subjected to slight statistical weighting procedures to calibrate the survey base to national demographic proportions. Households selected for inclusion in the survey sample received multiple callbacks to increase the probability of obtaining a representative distribution of adults.

"Born-again Christians" were defined in these surveys as people who said they have made "a personal commitment to Jesus Christ that is still important in their life today" and who also indicated they believe that when they die they will go to Heaven because they had confessed their sins and had accepted Jesus Christ as their savior. Respondents were *not* asked to describe themselves as "born again." Being classified as "born again" is not dependent upon church or denominational affiliation or involvement.

"Evangelicals" are considered a subset of born-again Christians in Barna surveys. In addition to meeting the born-again criteria, evangelicals also meet seven other conditions. Those include saying their faith is very important in their life today; contending that they have a personal responsibility to share their religious beliefs about Christ with non-Christians; stating that Satan exists; maintaining that eternal salvation is possible only through grace, not works; asserting that Jesus Christ lived a sinless life on earth; saying that the Bible is totally accurate in all it teaches; and describing God as the all-knowing, all-powerful, perfect deity who created the universe and still rules it today. Further, respondents were *not* asked to describe themselves as "evangelical." Being classified as "evangelical" is not dependent upon any church or denominational affiliation or involvement.

> Example:
>
> For the purposes of this example, we will use the average amount given by Protestants.
>
> *The Giving Church* has a membership of 650. This breaks down to 325 families or 425 adults. Each family donates $1,304 in tithes and pledges annually or $25.07 weekly. This equals $554,200.00 annual income for *the Giving Church*.
>
> *The Giving Church* has a senior pastor and one associate pastor, as well as an office manager and facilities caretaker. The salaries, benefits and insurance for this staff absorb approximately 40% of the total income. Do you think the balance is enough to cover the rent/mortgage, taxes, and general operating expenses as well as support the many ministries offered?

In order for your church to grow and remain viable you must support it. Would $554,200.00 be enough to operate your church for one full year?

You probably already figured that $1,304 annually equals 10% of a total take-home income of $13,040.00. If your income is greater than this, think about what you are giving. Are you giving at least the average $25.07 a week?

Where do you think your money is going?

_____
_____
_____
_____
_____
_____

Where would you like to see your money go?

_____
_____
_____
_____
_____

For the Congregation... for You!: Why do you make your current giving decisions?

The following exercise is to determine how you think about giving. Which of these categories best characterizes your current giving? You may select one or two that best represent your current practices. In order to change and develop your giving patterns, you first need to understand how and why you make your current decisions. Many of us have never given any thought to this process.

This is the beginning of changing your way of thinking!

How Your Giving Decisions Are Made

Category	Select 1 or 2
Thankful to God You are already giving 10% or more and/or giving what you can at this time. You are working toward giving more in the future.	
Lack of Motivation You feel that the church has failed to provide you with a compelling vision of how the church will make a difference in the community. You are willing to give more, but want more information.	
Investment You do not give to the church because you do not see a sufficient return on your investment. Ask yourself, "What am I looking for?" Then determine its value and give accordingly.	
Church Needs Your Money The church has done an inadequate job for your money. You remain oblivious to the church's expectations, needs and potential. Help your church develop better ways to communicate.	
Unaware of What the Bible Teaches You are not aware of what the Bible says about your responsibility to apply God's gifts and resources in ways that affect lives. Gain this information so your giving can increase.	
You Work Hard for Your Money You work hard for your money and figure it is yours to use as you please. Your priorities revolve around your personal needs and desires. Work on changing this way of thinking. Remember: Your blessings come from God.	

If you selected any category except "thankful to God," I am glad you are reading this book. Giving is just as much a part of your Christian life as is church attendance. Do not deny yourself the opportunity to receive greater fulfillment.

Good news… you have already begun the process of maturing and changing!

_____
_____
_____
_____
_____
_____
_____
_____
_____
_____
_____
_____
_____
_____
_____

For the Church:
Why do you think your congregation makes the giving decisions it makes?

Church leaders should take this exercise to understand how their congregation makes its giving decisions. Your answers should be based on the majority of people in your congregation. Select no more than two categories. When you've completed the exercise, ask a small group of your congregation – approximately 10-15 people – to do it also. Compare and discuss your findings.

Why Giving Decisions are Made

Category	Select 1 or 2
Thankful to God Majority are currently giving 10% or more and/or giving what they can at this time. They are working toward giving more in the future.	
Lack of Motivation It is felt that the church has failed to provide the congregation with a compelling vision of how it can make a difference in the community. People give but not as much as they can. Think about producing a monthly newsletter if you do not currently have one.	
Investment They do not give to the church because they do not see a sufficient return on their investment. What are you giving your congregation? Think about producing a monthly newsletter if you do not currently have one.	
The Church Needs Their Contributions You have done an inadequate job of asking for money. Your congregation remains oblivious to the church's expectations, needs and potential. How do you share financial information with your congregation? Think about preparing an annual report.	
Unaware of What the Bible Teaches The congregation is not aware of what the Bible says about its responsibility to apply God's gifts and resources in ways that affect lives. What are you preaching?	
They Work Hard for Their Money They work hard for their money and figure it is theirs to use as they please. Their priorities revolve around their personal needs and desires. What are you going to do about this? How can you get the people to understand that everything they have is a blessing from God?	

Take a look at how and why you are presently seeking support from your congregation.

Small intimate group settings, sometimes known as "cottage meetings," may be one way to help increase giving. Speaking to the masses from the pulpit is not always the best way to educate people on giving. Having cottage meetings, facilitated by laypersons, can quite often measure greater results.

Chapter 4
What do You Have to Give?

For the Congregation... for You!

Money... Time... Talent and Skills... In-Kind Services... Donations

There are several ways to give to your church:
- Money
- Time
- Talent and Skills
- In-Kind Services
- Donations

Before we can embark on the needs of your church, let us take a moment to look at you personally. Don't hide behind the thought of "I do not have," and therefore give nothing and do nothing. We all have something to give to our church and God. For some of us, it is just not very obvious. Money tends to be the most obvious.

The task is to figure out what it is that you can give. Before you can give to others, you must first know what you have to give. You need to review your personal financial situation and growth potential, as well as take a personal inventory.

Example:

Sally and Bill D'Mode prepared their personal inventories, and here is what they placed on their list:

Sally	**Bill**
Employed	Employed
Sewing	Carpenter
Crafts	Bowling
Loves talking to people	Loves talking to people

Here is how they put their inventory to good use within their church:

- They both tithe
- Sally loves to sew, so she made the curtains for the classrooms
- Bill is a carpenter and he made a ramp for the church entrance
- Sally organizes the Annual Holiday Bazaar for the women's group
- Bill bowls on the men's group monthly bowling league
- They both are members of the prayer chain

Look at the various ministries within your church and decide what you want to get involved in; determine where your talents can best be used. Consider your schedule and figure out how you can best give your time to your church.

Since you attend church, why not be involved in the welcoming committee? Or since you love to cook, perhaps you can cook for the monthly women's breakfast!

What is on your personal inventory? Develop one here.
Try to list at least five items or activities.

1. _____
2. _____

What do You Have to Give?

3. _____
4. _____
5. _____

Make a list of how you can use the items on your personal inventory for your church.

Try to list at least four different ways.

1. _____
2. _____
3. _____
4. _____

Is tithing or money on your list? If not, ask yourself why not.

In Genesis 14:20, Abraham gave tithes unto Melchizedek. Why did Abraham do this? The Bible does not tell us why. We are not told that God commanded him to do it; but the fact that he did tells us that he was acting in accordance with God's will. So stop looking for a reason to give! Give because it is right. Give because it feels good. Give because you love your church and wish to see it prosper and continue into the future for your children and your children's children. Stop looking for justification. And, most importantly, do not be concerned with what others are giving. Comparing can hinder you.

> **Deuteronomy 14:22**
> Thou shalt truly tithe all the increase of thy seed, that thy field bringeth forth year by year.

Do not give because you are looking for something in return.

Dr. Patterson writes: "One of the greatest injustices that many pastors have done to the church is to insist that God demands one-tenth of our income and one-seventh of our week. The implications are that the other nine-tenths of our income and the other six days of the week are ours to do with as we please. The real truth is that everything belongs to God! Not only the tithe, but everything else: 100% belongs to Him. We are simply stewards being obedient to our Heavenly Master – Jesus Christ, our Lord and Savior. The tithe is simply the basic starting-point in our Christian financial commitment."

Principle of Divine Ownership vs. the Principle of Dominion

> **Genesis 1:28**
> And God blessed them, and God said unto them, Be fruitful, and multiply, and replenish the earth, and subdue it: and have dominion over the fish of the sea, and over the fowl of the air, and over every living thing that moveth upon the earth.

Too often we base our entire relationship with our church on one Sunday morning service each week. If your giving practices are based on spending two to three hours a week in church, then you are probably not giving enough; you are also missing the greater picture and definitely not seeking the greatest rewards. Sunday services may include the sharing of the sacrament, a baptism, or a memorable lesson; but the church still does a great deal more for you, your family and the community than can be experienced within two to three hours.

Take a moment to list why you call upon your pastor and/or the church. Some examples may include christenings, weddings, confirmations, and funerals.

1. _____
2. _____
3. _____
4. _____

In order for the church to perform any of these activities, it needs money and assistance. Many people complain that the church "charges" for everything. Unfortunately, many do not have a choice. They cannot turn on the electricity for free. If people gave proportionally to what they receive, perhaps these additional life events would not have an extra cost. Many of us spend hundreds of dollars on the limousines for our wedding; and thousands for the reception, not to mention a few hundred for the flowers, but grumble over giving the church a couple hundred dollars to host the wedding ceremony itself.

Dr. Patterson's paper continues by discussing how God has given humanity the exclusive right or dominion to rule over His property and world. How we have not only been given the right of dominion, but we are also "free moral agents," able to make our own decisions and to determine our own actions. Therefore, we can bless God with our actions – or curse God with our actions. Obedience blesses God, while disobedience is a reproach unto God. Tithing blesses, while not tithing is a reproach.

If the principle of "divine ownership" could finally be understood, Dr. Patterson writes, then the problems associated with giving and tithing would be over within the hearts of all Christians.

The principle of divine ownership teaches us that there is nothing that does not belong to God; and the principle of dominion teaches us that humanity has been given stewardship over God's property.

The following is a list of several different ways you can give to your church. You may not have some of these items, but they are all obtainable.

_____

_____
_____
_____
_____

10 Ways for you to give to your church

1
Money

For some of us, it appears that money is the hardest thing to give. We don't think we have much. That's because we tend to see money as what is in our pockets, what is recorded in the check book register, or what is posted to our savings account statement. Gifts of money go far beyond those perceptions.

Say you decide to give 10% of your annual income to your church. You can do this many different ways:

- Give exactly the same amount each week.

- Give what you can each week as long as it totals your pledge amount at the end of the year.

- Pay your tithes monthly, quarterly, or annually.

- I say: do what works best for you!

> **Malachi 3:10**
> Bring ye all the tithes into the storehouse, that there may be meat in mine house, and prove me now herewith, saith the Lord of hosts, if I will not open you the windows of heaven, and pour you out a blessing, that there shall not be room enough to receive it.

God wants a cheerful giver. If you are stressing over the right way to give, you are not cheerful. In fact, the giving can take on a negative connotation within your life, which in many cases alters what is given.

> Example:
>
> Sally earns $40,000 annually. Her annual tithe is $4,000, or 10%. She works September through June, and spends July and August at home with her family. During the months of September through June, Sally gives $375.00 each month to her church, and during July and August she gives $125.00 each month. At the end of the year, Sally has still met her promised amount of $4,000. Sally

decreases her giving during July and August because her income drops for those months.

> **Proverbs 3:9**
> Honor the Lord with thy substance, and with the first fruits of all thine increase.

Look at your individual situation. Giving should come from the heart. Be a cheerful giver. Do not allow the giving to place a burden upon you. Listen to how God leads you to give. Listen to what God tells you to give. There are many ways to give money to your church.

Cash Gifts: Pledging Offerings and Tithes

Why do we list both offerings and tithes? We consider *tithes* to be your base pledge. The goal is to give 10%. To start, you may be giving less than that amount, with a goal of working toward that mark. Your *offering* is above and beyond your tithe. Perhaps at Easter you might wish to give an additional $100.00, or you may want to give something toward a specific ministry.

Your tithes are usually not earmarked. However, you may want to specify how you want your money used; this can be done through additional cash donations. In fact, I recommend that all large cash donations be earmarked. This way you can be sure that your gift will be used as intended.

"Why should I tell the church in advance what I plan to give? Why can't I just give them what I can afford each week?"

If you did not know how much money you were going to be paid each week, each month, or on an annual basis, how would you be able to plan? You couldn't! The church needs you to pledge annually so that it, too, can plan.

What do You Have to Give?

> "Plan what?"
> *Everything!*

Without knowing approximately how much money is coming in, the church cannot plan for even the simplest things such as printing the Sunday bulletin. Also, making a pledge gives you the opportunity to think about what your church means to you, and to place a value on that meaning.

2
Last Will and Testament

Do you have a will? A will is a sure way to guarantee that your possessions and valuables end up where you want them to go. Be specific about the allocation of your valuables, money, property, and do not forget your church. In preparing your will, it is not only money that can be left to the church and your loved ones, but can include rare books, antiques, furnishings, property, etc. You can stipulate that your church retain certain items for its own use or sell them at auction, retaining the proceeds. You can even stipulate how these proceeds can be spent.

Long-term investments
Stock and bonds
Property
Mutual funds

What will happen to these investments when you die? Take control! Make decisions while you have your health and mental alertness. By leaving clear instruction regarding your family and church, you are pleasing God on all accounts.

> Example:
>
> Bill and Sally D'Mode have the following investments and possessions:
> - A house
> - Stocks in various companies
> - Bill's 401(k)

- Sally's 401(k)
- Savings and money market accounts
- A few pieces of antique furniture

Bill and Sally have drafted a simple will stating that:
- The church will receive 25% of the net proceeds from the sale of the house
- The church will receive the antique desk and chair
- All other investments are divided among their children

While reviewing a church's financials, I examined its list of bequests. I was amazed to see how some of them dated back over 100 years, and still had remaining balances today. Some of the bequests had specific instructions and/or purposes, such as:

- Principal not to be used, but dividends to be used for altar flowers and Sunday school supplies.

- Funds to be used to help pay the pastor's salary.

- Funds to be used for major capital repairs and building restoration.

- Residence sold and net proceeds for church building repairs.

Generally, churches are not in the profit-making business. However, they do not want to operate in the red. Breaking even is quite frequently the annual goal, at worst. But, with long-term contributions, you can help your church operate not only in the black, but do so for many years to come.

Be generous with your money and possessions. Providing for your church in your will is an action that will cost you nothing today.

3
Time
Who has time?

For some, it is easier and quicker to write a check than it is to give their time. Giving your time to the church can be a greater sacrifice.

With both parents working, and the shuffling of our children to their daily activities, there is not much left in the way of free time! Still, it is important that you give not only your money but your time to God and the church. Saying that you are a Christian but never going to church is a life out of balance. If you work on Sundays, find out if your church offers additional services, either on a Saturday or one day/evening during the week. If you cannot make it to church because of your work schedule, it should be in your personal mission statement for you to find a church that has services at a time you can attend.

> **Exodus 35:29**
> The children of Israel brought a willing offering unto the Lord, every man and woman, whose heart made them willing to bring for all manner of work, which the Lord had commanded to be made by the hand of Moses.

Stop making excuses, give your time to God, and go to church! Showing up every Easter does not constitute a "regular basis."

How much time do you spend watching TV? Do you sleep until noon on Sunday? We can all look at our schedules and find pockets of free time. Give some of that time to the church, to God. In many cases, you will not have to look very far.

Example:

At Sally and Bill's church, a different family is out front greeting and welcoming the worshipers and newcomers. Their church was looking for additional families to be a part of this ministry. The commitment was one Sunday every three months at the 9:00 am service, and to arrive no later than 8:30 am on that Sunday. Since they were already at church, this donation of time did not add to their present scheduled but enhanced their church experience.

Find hidden ways within your church to give. My church has liturgical dancers. One of the ways I give my time is by dancing.

Below is a short list of ways you can give your time.

Sample Gifts of Time
Get involved with the Christmas pageant
Teach Sunday school
Help compile the weekly bulletin
Help type the monthly newsletter
Bring the Eucharist to the homebound
Visit the sick
Join the greeters and welcome ministry
Help clean the church grounds
Organize the church picnic
Be an usher
Join the prayer chain
Plant flowers

4
Talents and Skills

The talents and skills we have are God's blessings. What are your talents and skills? Before you say, "I don't have any talents or skills," ask your friends to tell you what you are good at. Sometimes others see in us what we do not see in ourselves.

Take a moment and list your talents and skills here:

1._____

2._____

What do You Have to Give?

3._____
4._____
5._____

Churches do not just need money or people with free time; they also need people with talents and skills. Look at the list of talents and skills you wrote above. Can you see how your church can use you?

> Example:
>
> Bill D'Mode is a carpenter. Over the past months, Bill has noticed that several of the elderly are having trouble walking up the front steps to the church. Bill decided that he could build a small ramp that would not obstruct the general flow of traffic but still make it easier for the elderly.

How can your talents and skills help your church?

Sample List of Talent and Skills
Have a beautiful voice? Sing in the choir!
Play an instrument? Play in the band!
Love to sew? Make curtains for the classrooms!
Good at organizing? Organize the annual bazaar!

5
In-Kind Services

Sometimes the best donations are those that are needed by the church. Below is a list of such items. Review this list. Check with your church; perhaps it can use some of the items on this list. Ask what other services would be useful.

When financial times are tight, these gifts and services can be a saving grace to the church and to you. It can give you a sense belonging and fulfillment, while filling a need for the church.

Sample In-Kind Services
Web site development/design/maintenance
Videotape production
Computer set-up
Help paint a room or the whole church
If your church has a thrift shop, offer to volunteer
Carpentry work
Typing services
Design posters/flyers
Lawn care and landscaping
Accounting/finance

#6
Donations

Donations are another way to give to your church. There are several ways to donate.

1. You can donate items that you presently own, but no longer need or use.

2. You can donate your time to assist with a project or ministry.

3. If you own a company you can make a financial donation.

The value of the donation is not what's important; it is the thought of doing it that counts.

Sample Donations
Items for the kitchen
Books and Bibles
Office supplies
If your church has a thrift shop, donate clothes
Buying a new car or van? Why not donate the old
one to the church?
Purchasing a new piano? Donate the old one to the church!

7
Giving begins at home

Even the youngest of children can understand giving. Usually, young children do not have money of their own to give, but they do have time and talents.

Teach your children to be involved, to give of their time and talents. Allow them to see *your* involvement. Do not think that your son or daughter does not see your involvement, or is not proud of you, just because they do not tell you about it directly. Listen instead to what they tell their friends!

> One Saturday afternoon, my son had two friends over to play. I happen to walk by his room when I heard him say to them, "My mom dances and choreographs at our church." One friend replied, "Wow, that's cool! My mom doesn't even get us up to go to church!"

In today's world, where there are so many things vying for our children's time on a Sunday morning – soccer, baseball, ice skating, hockey and so forth – teach your children that their ability to perform in these activities is a blessing from God, and that they need to make time in the busy schedules to give back to God. If your child loves to sing, have them join the youth choir. Perhaps you work, like I do, and cannot get your child to after-school activities at the church. There are still many other ways they can get involved. One church that my family and I belonged to had youth ushers. My son was part of this ministry. Every four to six weeks, he ushered. This was the one Sunday where he really cared about what he wore!

Giving should be a family affair. Openly show your generosity around your children. It is important for our children to see that giving is something we do joyfully and willfully.

8
Value the pastor
Believe in and support your pastor… your messenger.

What would you hear without the pastor?
You cannot truly hear God's word without the preacher!

Give back to your pastor. Like any garden, if you do not love it, water it, and feed it, the growth will be minimal. Part of your selecting the church you attend should be your belief in and respect for the pastor. If you do not like the preacher, what are you receiving? Not much, because you are spending too much time thinking about your feelings! Close them out and hear the Word. Allow this person to take you to another level. Your giving will not increase as long as you are harboring negative feelings.

> Recently, I had a conversation with a young man about church. He was actually reading a few pages of this book while I was writing it. I asked him if he went to church and he replied, "I used to, but don't any more." Without trying to get too personal, I asked him why not. He began

to tell me a story of how the pastor and deacon disappointed him, and how after the incident he never went back to church. I explained to him that he has allowed two people to control him and remove him from the church, a church that he said he loved. I explained to him that the church belongs to God. He asked me what he should do because he really did not want to go back to that church. I told him to find a new church. Do you know that he never realized that he had that option?

We have plenty of excuses for not going to church. If there is a problem with every church you attend, perhaps the problem is not with the church.

#9
Resources
We all have "resources."

Who do you know? Where do you work? Perhaps the church needs new carpet and your sister is a carpet salesperson. She is your resource. Having an anniversary celebration? Do you know someone at the local newspaper who can send a photographer to the celebration? This would be your resource.

10
When should you stop giving?
Never! If something goes wrong, something happens in your church that you do not like, do not respond by withholding your tithes or stopping your involvement. Speak to the appropriate people. If this does not work, or is not an option, perhaps it is time to find a new church worthy of your gifts. However, in doing this, remember that the grass is not *always* greener on the other side. Also remember that you don't have to like everything. As adults we should be able to handle a little diversity within our lives.

Jumping from church to church will not give your heart, mind, and faith adequate time to truly engage. Try to stick it out, get involved and help effect change. Just one last point: If you must leave… leave with dignity. You may want to return one day.

Chapter 5
Understanding Your Personal Financial Situation

For the Congregation... for You!

In assessing your church and your current level of giving and activities within the church, please remember that this is a personal task. This book is not about finding the perfect solution. It is about finding your personal balance – the balance that works for you at your income level, within your lifestyle, without causing you undue stress.

This is your personal financial profile. You do not have to share it with anyone; just be honest with yourself. If you are married, you can do this individually (comparing profiles when done) or you can do this together. How you do this exercise depends on how you currently manage your finances.

Why do we ask that you date this profile? It is hoped that after you complete this book, you may change your giving patterns. You can make positive changes and experience growth!

> The way in which you handle your finances will mark your spiritual commitment to God! It is often said that more could be learned about a person's commitment to Christ by looking at his checkbook rather than his prayer book.
>
> Dr. Rick L. Patterson, Th.D.
> The Law of Tithing

Understanding Your Personal Financial Situation

What is your current level of giving to the church?

In order to be consistent throughout your financial profile, you need to decide if your calculations and answers are based on before-tax or after-tax dollars. As mentioned earlier, we do not offer a decision here; discuss this with your pastor if you are in need of guidance.

Please select one: ☐ Before-Tax   ☐ After-Tax

Total Annual Giving
What is your current level of monetary giving to the church?

☐ 10% tithing   What is this in dollars annually? $ _____

☐ Less than 10%   What is this in dollars annually? $ _____

☐ More than 10%   What is this in dollars annually? $ _____

Giving Profile

1. Your annual gross income: $_____. This is your income before taxes, 401(k), medical, etc. have been taken out.

2. Your annual net income: $_____. This is your income after taxes, 401(k), medical, etc. have been taken out. This represents the total amount you actually take home.

3. How much are you currently giving to your church? You should fill in only one of the following four areas:

   Weekly: $_____   Biweekly: $_____

   Monthly: $_____   Annually: $_____

4. Are you giving for more than one adult? ☐Yes ☐No
   If yes, how many? _____

5. How many children are included in your giving? _____

6. Is your giving divided among more than one church?
   ☐Yes ☐No (If no, please skip).

   If yes, how much goes to each church?

   $_____ of giving that goes to church 1: _____
   (Annual amount)   (Name of church)

   $_____ of giving that goes to church 2: _____
   (Annual amount)   (Name of church)

   $_____ of giving that goes to church 3: _____
   (Annual amount)   (Name of church)

7. What percent of your giving does this represent? _____

8. Why do you give to more than one church? _____

_____

_____

_____

_____

_____

_____

_____

_____

Understanding Your Personal Financial Situation

Now look at what you wrote for the "Total Annual Giving"
$ _____

What is the total number of people you are donating for?
_____
(Total adults and children)

**Divide the Total Annual Giving
by
Total adults and children**

Put this answer here: $ _____
(This represents how much you are giving per person annually)

Do you really believe that this amount is equal to what you and your family receives? ☐Yes ☐No

Example:

Figures for a family of three people
(mother, father and child)

$1,305 Total Annual Giving = $435 (rounded up) per person annually/$36.25 monthly

If you answered no above, how can you change this?

_____
_____
_____
_____

What do you do when you get a raise?

_____
_____
_____
_____

Here is what Sally does when she gets a raise:

Example:

Sally got a $3,200 raise for the year. She gives to her church based on her gross salary. Therefore, her church contribution will increase by $320, or 10% annually. Also Sally has a 401(k). Each year she increases her 401(k) by 2% until she reaches the maximum. After taxes, social security, medical benefits etc., the rest is hers. She feels good about this because she has paid both God and herself first.

Whatever you get, pay God and yourself first!

> **Acts 20:35**
> I have shewed you all things, how that so laboring ye ought to support the weak, and to remember the words of the Lord Jesus, how he said, It is more blessed to give than to receive.

If you cannot start at 10%, then start at 2%, 3%, 5%... just *start*! Build it each year as your salary increases. If you are at a job where the salary does not increase each year, you should begin to look at this situation and pray for guidance.

Understanding Your Personal Budget

The following budget is very detailed in order to help you get a full picture of your total income and spending habits. You can multiply the total monthly column by 12 to get your annual figures. Write this figure.

Understanding Your Personal Financial Situation

We are not trying to teach you to save. If you need assistance in that area, there are several books and Web sites available on budgeting and how to increase saving. This is your first step in learning how to increase your giving to the church by clearly seeing what is coming in and going out. See where you are spending and determine if you are giving proportionally to your church.

Personal Income Worksheet

Personal Budget INCOME	You	Spouse	Total Monthly	Total Annual
Full time job #1				
Full time job #2				
Part time job #1				
Part time job #2				
Alimony Child Support				
Interest/Dividends				
Trust Funds				
Other Income:				

> **Acts 2:44**
> And all that believed were together, and had all things common.

Personal Expense Worksheet

EXPENSES	You	Spouse	Monthly	Annual
Personal Savings				
Church Contribution				
Mortgage/Rent				
Property Taxes				
Gas/Electric				
Water/Sewer				
Credit Cards				
Personal & Student Loans				
Daily Lunch/Snack				
Doctor Visits/Prescriptions				
Cell & Home Phone				
Child Care				
Auto Payment/Maintenance				
Transportation				
Tuition/Books				
Household Items				
Groceries				
Personal Items				
Cable/Internet				
Alimony/Child Support				
Clothing				
Insurance				
Pets				
Entertainment & Gifts				
Other Donations/Misc.				

Understanding Your Personal Financial Situation

Tracking Your Monthly Expenses

If you are unable to list your expenses because you have never tracked them before, then the following exercise is for you! On the tracking worksheet, you should indicate how much you spend for each category on a weekly basis. This will help you to derive your monthly totals.

Monthly Expense Tracking Worksheet

EXPENSES	Week 1	Week 2	Week 3	Week 4	Total Month
Personal Savings					
Church Contribution					
Mortgage/Rent					
Property Taxes					
Gas/Electric					
Water/Sewer					
Credit Cards					
Personal & Student Loans					
Daily Lunch/Snack					
Doctor Visits/Prescriptions					
Cell & Home Phone					
Child Care					
Auto Payment/Maintenance					
Transportation					
Tuition/Books					
Household Items					
Groceries					
Personal Items					
Cable/Internet					
Alimony/Child Support					
Clothing					
Insurance					
Pets					
Entertainment & Gifts					
Other Donations/Misc.					

Financial management tools are another way to help you keep track of your spending. By using these tools, not only will your accounting be more accurate, it will make it easier for you to do this over time.

> **Deuteronomy 16:17**
> Every man shall give as he is able, according to the blessing of the Lord thy God which he hath given thee.

Financial Notes and Plans

Making changes in how we save, spend, and give to the church is not an easy task. Do not expect to have all the answers when you complete this book. It may take you months to get it all figured out. The point is that you are on the road to growth and maturity in how you manage your finances and give to the church. Take notes, make plans and write them down. Adjust them as needed and review them on a regular basis.

_____
_____
_____
_____
_____
_____
_____
_____
_____
_____

Chapter 6
Understanding the Needs of the Church

For the Congregation... for You!

Let us take a general look at the needs of the church.

We will start with our example church.

The Giving Church has a total of 650 registered members. This breaks down to 425 families. If each family gave $20 per week, with an extra $25 at Easter and $25 at Christmas, *the Giving Church* would have $463,250 annually.

For a church, this can be a nominal amount. After salaries, insurance and rent, over 50-60% is most likely gone.

How do you make your decision about how much to give? If you are only looking at what you see each Sunday at church, you are not making your giving decision based on total services offered and available. Sometimes the availability of services is greater than the actual usage of those services. Base your giving on what is available.

> The Reverend Linda Hunt of Living Word Christian Fellowship stated in a sermon, "Your best can sometimes be greater than the 10% given by those who this comes easy to."

When you give, you are not only helping to pay the bills, but you are investing in the church – today and tomorrow. Your contributions help keep the doors open.

In figuring out how much to give, do not think about what others are giving or who may have more than you. Focus on your blessings and your convictions. During tough times, do the best you can, but do not stop giving.

Understanding the Needs of the Church

If you are unsure about what to give, or do not understand how to calculate it, the following chart can help you figure it out.

Giving Chart

Gross Annual Income	Gross Weekly Income	Weekly Giving 5%	Weekly Giving 7.50%	Weekly Tithe 10%
20,000.00	384.61	19.23	28.85	38.46
25,000.00	480.76	24.04	36.06	48.08
30,000.00	576.92	28.85	43.27	57.69
35,000.00	673.07	33.65	50.48	67.31
40,000.00	769.23	38.46	57.69	76.92
45,000.00	865.38	43.27	64.90	86.54
50,000.00	961.53	48.08	72.11	96.15
55,000.00	1,057.68	52.88	79.33	105.77
60,000.00	1,153.84	57.69	86.54	115.38
65,000.00	1,250.00	62.50	93.75	125.00
70,000.00	1,346.15	67.31	100.96	134.62
75,000.00	1,442.30	72.12	108.17	144.23
80,000.00	1,358.46	67.92	101.88	135.85
85,000.00	1,634.61	81.73	122.60	163.46
90,000.00	1,730.76	86.54	129.81	173.08
95,000.00	1,826.92	91.35	137.02	182.69
100,000.00	1,923.07	96.15	144.23	192.31

How well do you know your church?

Some people go to church week after week and do not know what goes on beyond what happens during the time they are there. That is not being a member. That is what is called a "permanent visitor." Below is a list of questions for you to answer.

They all pertain to the general activities within your church.

If you do not know the answer to a particular question, make a note of it so that you can get the answer at a later time. If you are new to your church (less than three months) wait a while before doing this questionnaire.

> **Exodus 25:21**
> And thou shalt put the mercy seat above upon the ark: and in the ark thou shalt put the testimony that I shall give thee

Questionnaire: How well do you know your church?

Question	Answer
How many services are held each Sunday?	
What are the times for these services?	
When is Sunday school offered?	
Are weekday services offered?	
Are there adult education classes?	
Does your church have a Web site?	
Can you make your tithe/offering over the Internet?	
Is there a monthly newsletter/calendar of events?	
Does your church have an annual meeting?	
Are the financial details offered freely?	
Are the elders/vestry voted for by the congregation?	
How long is their term?	
If not voted for, how are they appointed?	
Is there a people's warden?	
Is there an annual ministry fair?	
What ministries are available for children?	
Is a family/household profile required annually?	
Is the church anniversary celebrated annually?	
If yes, when?	
Is the pastors' anniversary celebrated annually?	
If yes, when?	
Is there an information bulletin board?	
Is there an annual picnic?	

How did you do?

1 – 3 blanks: You know your church very well. Review what you did not know and make it a point of getting the information.

4 – 7 blanks: You seem to know some things, but still need to know more. Make it a point to learn the information you did not know.

8 – 10 blanks: You are not very aware of many of the activities within your church. Is there a pattern to what you do not know? For instance: Perhaps you do not have any children, and therefore, are not aware of programs for youth. Work toward increasing your knowledge.

Over 10 blanks: You attend church, but are in a vacuum. Work toward expanding your knowledge about your church.

On your next visit to church, bring a small pad. You should look around and take in the environment, watch the people – your fellow parishioners. Read the bulletin board. Make a note of everything that appears new to you or unfamiliar. It is amazing what we hear and see when we open ourselves to the environment around us. We should not walk into the church and go directly to our seat without seeing the world around us. Yet many of us do! When we segregate ourselves, that segregation controls how we think and therefore ultimately what we give.

> **Psalms 24:1**
> The earth is the Lord's, and the fullness thereof; the world, and they that dwell therein.

Yours, Mine & God's

Chapter 7
Let the Church Speak

For the Church

Before you can ask your congregation to give, you must know what you have to offer. Your first exercise will be to develop a profile for your church. Each year, many activities take place within your church. Some are more visible than others. Some, though not visible to all, are assumed to be happening (weddings, funerals and confirmation); but there are many other activities the general congregation does not know about (private counseling sessions, for example).

Annual Report

One of the easiest ways to create a church profile is by developing an annual report. Having an annual report is one way to ensure that a concise listing of all activities is recorded. The report should be distributed to your congregation at your annual meeting. If your church does not hold an annual meeting, perhaps this is an activity that you might like to consider. Either way, set a particular time of the year – preferably January – to distribute this report.

What should be in the annual report?

- Opening letter from the senior clergy
- Report of each associate clergy's year in review
- Church statistics
- List of activities and ministries
- Report from each ministry leader
- Financial profile
- Additional special reports, such as explanation of major expenses not in original budget (a flood created the need for a new floor in the church office, for example).

The purpose of the annual report and meeting is twofold:

- The year in review
  Looking back on the previous year: actual income and expenses

- The year ahead
  Looking at what is planned for the coming year: planned budget and activities

The benefits of producing an annual report and holding an annual meeting can be:

- Greater understanding of where the money goes
- Possible increase in giving and participation
- Fewer questions are raised during the year
- People can plan

If you choose to have an annual meeting, try to have it the same time each year, such as the third Sunday in January. State that the meeting will only last a specified time (two hours is reasonable). This will help people to plan their day. Make sure you stick to the length of time you have allotted.

Many churches do not present this information to their congregation. If you do not want to prepare a full detailed reporting of each program/ministry, I recommend that you at least present a summary breakdown of general operating income and expenses.

A faithful church (congregation) is one that pulls together financially. However, even the faithful have questions. How often can you ask for money to meet the budget before people begin to question the management of the church finances? If you are asking for additional money more than twice a year, I guarantee you that people are asking questions – if not of you, than of themselves and their friends. Avoid this. Be proactive and offer the information.

The annual report statistics will carry forward into the next year as a starting-point for your growth and development. Patterns of growth and/or decline can be easily analyzed from this report.

Aside from the above outline of activities, each ministry should prepare a report of the previous year's activities. This report serves to communicate the importance and viability of each ministry to your congregation. People do not participate in the unknown. Telling people the successes of each ministry and the difficulties these ministries face can create involvement and interest.

The next two steps in developing your annual report involve putting together your financial profile and list of activities and ministries. As activities are developed, this list will change. As activities are discontinued, this list will change.

If you choose to not produce an annual report, you should have a process in place where your congregation can feel free to ask questions about the finances. Your goal is to make the information available.

> **Exodus 25:2**
> Speak unto the children of Israel, that they bring me an offering: of every man that giveth it willingly with his heart ye shall take my offering.

Following is an outline of the statistics for your annual report. This report will reflect how you ended the previous year, and show a comparison against this year.

Annual Report Statistics Worksheet

Annual Report Statistics --Description	Last Year	This Year
Number of Parishioners		
Number of Households		
Number of Married Couples		
Number of Single Adults		
Number of Children through age 5		
Number of Children grades 1 - 5		
Number of Children grades 6 - 8		
Number of Children grades 9 - 12		
Number of Young Adults in College		
Number of Transfers In (New Members)		
Number of Transfers Out		
Number of Sunday Services		
Services of Holy Eucharist		
Average Sunday Attendance (52 weeks)		
Number of Saturday Services		
Number of Weekday Services		
Number of Weekday Services of Holy Eucharist		
Number of Private services of Holy Communion		
Services of Holy Baptism		
Number of Persons Baptized		
Number of Persons Receiving First Communion		
Number of Persons Confirmed		
Number of Burial Services		
Number of Weddings		

Financial Profile

This is probably one of the most important sections of the annual report. Everyone wants to know where the money is coming from and how it is being spent. It is always good to have a written narrative prepared to go along with the financial information. Oral and/or software-aided presentations can also assist in helping your congregation understand the information and numbers.

When presenting your budget in your annual report, remember that it doesn't have to be this detailed. You can prepare a summary. If you choose to only present a summary, make sure it does not incite too many questions. If it does, your staff will now be burdened with explaining the budget. The main task here is to make your congregation aware of what it costs to operate the church, and how their tithes/offerings are being used. Help them to understand why they should continue to give and give more.

Further, if you operate a school, thrift shop or any other type of business, please note that each of these entities should have independent budgets. However, you should still present one overall budget that encompasses each of the independent operations.

Financial Profile Income Worksheet

Budget Accounts - INCOME	Last Year Planned	Last Year Actual	This year Planned
Tithe Offerings			
Plate Offerings (not in envelopes)			
Pledge Above or Without Tithes			
Unpledged Envelope Giving			
Easter Offering			
Christmas Offering			
New Year's Offering			
Pastor Gifts			
Flower Funds			
Music Income			
Coffee Hour Income			
Annual Fundraising Event			
Youth Group Fundraising			
Rental Income			
Community Outreach Programs			
Endowment/Investment Income			
Church School Offering			
Specials Program Income			
Misc. Income			
Total Income			

There are many income and expenses that your church can have, so make sure that you include them in your budget. If your church has a parish house, rectory or any additional property, make sure that you include the income and operating expenses for them as well.

_____

_____

_____

_____

_____

Financial Profile Expense Worksheet

Budget Account - EXPENSES	Last Year Planned	Last Year Actual	This Year Planned
Staff Expenses			
Mortgage/Lease			
Diocesan Assessment			
Water/Sewer			
Gas/Electricity			
Telephone			
Insurance			
Church Van/Car Expenses			
Office Operating/Equipment			
Altar Guild			
Music Expenses			
Security			
Facility Maintenance			
Garbage Collection			
Alarm System			
Hospitality & Coffee Hour			
Fundraising Events			
Youth Group			
Sunday School/Christian Education			
Community Outreach Expenses			
Advertisement			
Convention Expenses			
Pastors Discretionary Fund			
Visiting Ministers			
Misc. Expenses			
TOTAL EXPENSES			

Profile of Activities and Ministries

What does your church have to offer? Do not assume that your parishioners know! With several churches in town, you need to be clear on not only your mission, but on what you have to offer to your congregation and the community.

Your church can grow only if its people are involved. Make your available activities and ministries public.

Developing of a church profile of activities and ministries is a very simple task.

Step #1: On the list of activities and ministries, check off all the activities and ministries that are offered within your church during the current year. There are blank spaces for you to add in activities/ministries that are not on this list.

Step #2: Next indicate the percent of your congregation that you believe are aware of these activities.

Step #3: Indicate the percent of your congregation you believe is involved within each activity.

Step #4: Review your answers in step three and determine if there are enough people to properly support this ministry. Highlight each ministry where you feel participation is low.

If the people running the ministries have been doing so for five years or more, you may need to think about developing replacements. After about five years, some people need a change. What else can these people do? Put a checkmark next to all the ministries that fall within this category.

The person analyzing the following report should separate the analysis into two parts. Choose from the groupings below:

Part I
Successful programs with longevity
Participation is high, and the majority of the ministry leaders have been involved for four or fewer years.

Successful programs, but may need new leadership
Programs have been running successfully for five or more years under the same leadership. It is time to develop new leadership... just in case one of your current leaders wishes to retire, learn new things, expand their thinking or has simply developed an interest in another ministry.

Part II
Involvement is low, but it's a good program and vital to the community
Although involvement is low, this is an important ministry. You need to work on developing the leaders for this program first, and then increase participation.

Involvement is low and the return to the community is minimal
These programs may be placing a strain on your staff and congregation. You may want to consider placing some of these on the back burner for a while. Perhaps they need to be redeveloped, or can merge with another ministry.

This is a good exercise for your associate pastors to do. Ask each of them to do the exercise independently. Then have one person analyze the results and disclose the answers. This will help you to determine if your staff members are all on the same track.

_____
_____
_____

Activities and Ministries Awareness Worksheet

Profile of Activities and Ministries	Currently Offered	% Congregation Awareness	% Congregation Involved
After-School Activities			
Altar Guild			
Anniversary Celebration			
Building Maintenance			
Capital Campaign			
Christmas Pageant (Annual)			
Church Picnic (Annual)			
Daughters of the King			
Day Care			
Evangelism			
Fellowship Activities			
Greeters/Ushers			
Healing Mission			
Hospitality			
Lay Eucharistic Leaders			
Long-Range Planning			
Men's Group			
Music Ministries			
Outreach/Thrift Shop			
Pastoral Care			
Security			
Seniors Ministry			
Singles Ministry			
Special Programs			
Stewardship Committee			
Sunday School			
Thrift Shop			
Women's Group			
Youth Group			

_____

_____

_____

Closure Report

When an activity is discontinued or deemed not a success, a closure report should be prepared. The purpose of this report is to help ensure that ministries and/or programs can be reviewed or redeveloped for the future.

Knowing why a program is discontinued, or never made it off the ground, is just as important as understanding why a particular program is successful.

Ministry and Program Closure Report

Name of Activity/Ministry: _____

Activity/ Ministry Leader (s): _____

Date Started: _____ Date Ended: _____ ☐ Never Started

Purpose of Activity/Ministry:

_____
_____
_____
_____
_____
_____
_____
_____

Reason for Discontinuing or Canceling Activity/Ministry

(Select all that apply)

☐ Lack of Participation and/or Interest

☐ Lack of Leadership

☐ Lack of funding to start

☐ Space/Facility Problem

☐ Too expensive to continue

☐ Weather

In the following space be as thorough as possibility in explaining why this program was discontinued or cancelled:

_____
_____
_____
_____
_____
_____
_____
_____
_____
_____
_____

Person completing this report: _____ Date: _____

Fun, Fun, Fun and Fundraising

Have fun increasing your financial growth! Make sure that you assign cheerful, well-organized people to head your fundraising and stewardship events. Many churches do not host fundraising events because they believe that people should give from the heart. Although I agree with this, I also feel that fundraising events are critical to successful financial growth for any not-for-profit organization. You do not have to call them fundraising events; they can be called many things, such as: capital campaigns, annual giving campaign, and stewardship events. It does not matter what you call them, the idea is to plan the event.

Capital Campaign

When was the last time you had a capital campaign? Have you ever had a capital campaign? The purpose of a capital campaign is twofold:

1. Raise a substantial amount of money within a set period of time. Money raised is usually for major purchases such as the restoration of a bell-tower or the purchase of a new building.

2. Increase awareness that additional monies are needed from the congregation and community.

Quite frequently, grants are also awarded. Having a well-organized capital campaign can help in presenting your church to grantee organizations.

It is important to make sure that your parishioners understand that what they give to the capital campaign is beyond their regular tithes/offering.

Ministry Fair

Do you host an annual ministry fair? If you do not, here is another idea you may want to try.

What is a ministry fair? A ministry fair is an activity where each ministry sets up a table or booth to display information about its respective ministry. The booth/table can contain flyers, posters, presentations – and, most importantly, a sign-up sheet and list of planned events for the coming year. The best time for the fair is June, right before people leave for their summer vacations. In the early fall, each ministry leader should reach out to everyone who signed up for their ministry.

Schedule the fair for a time where people do not have to make a separate trip. One of the best times is right after church services on Sunday morning.

Make sure that you begin promoting the fair well in advance. So many functions fail due to the lack of time to properly promote and gather interest.

> **Luke 6:38**
> Give, and it shall be given unto you; good measure, pressed down, and shaken together, and running over, shall men give into your bosom. For with the same measure that ye mete withal it shall be measured to you again.

Committee Development

Many functions require a committee to organize and manage them. The most successful committees are those organized by a chairperson who clearly understands the event and has the personality to engage people in activities. Announcing that a volunteer is needed to head up a committee may at times get you somebody, but will this be the best person for this task?

If you have done a good job of knowing your parishioners, you can select your chairperson based upon recognized talents and skills, and then have them seek co-chairs and committee members. Even with this,

I prefer to be more direct and have a more personal approach. I enjoy telling people why I chose them for a particular committee of task.

> A few years ago, I chaired the 300th Anniversary for St. Peter's Episcopal Church in Freehold, NJ. Along with Father Frank, we selected a core group of people for the chair-committee. We selected these individuals based upon the various areas of responsibility we needed covered. Of the seven people we invited to be a part of the chair-committee, two were unable to accept due to other commitments, yet they were still able to be a part of the planning by handling very specific tasks. When someone says they are to busy too sit on a committee, but would still like to be involved, you need to know immediately how you want to use them.

Commitment

I always make it clear to the committee members what type of commitment is required of them. This can be anything from selling a certain number of tickets to bringing in gifts for an auction.
If people are unable to commit, thank them for their time and offer to call them again. Having a committee of people who are not committed will greatly alter the outcome of the event. If you settle, you will find yourself chairing a committee of one… you!

> **Romans 12:2**
> And be not conformed to this world: but be ye transformed by the renewing of your mind, that ye may prove what [is] that good, and acceptable, and perfect, will of God.

Yours, Mine & God's

Chapter 8
Getting the Word Out

For the Church

Communications

How well do you communicate with your congregation? When things happen within the church, are they discussed with the congregation, or do you rely on rumors for communication?

Communication within any organization is one of the most difficult areas to manage. What you disclose versus what you choose not to disclose is very important. Stating too much can cause as much damage as not stating enough. When you do not disclose enough information, you leave it up to your congregation to speculate. And quite frequently, when you disclose too much, you open yourself up to rumor.

The major concern here is how well you communicate. This book is filled with ideas of things you can do to help increase the receiving levels within the church. However, if your communication

> **Numbers 18:21**
> And, behold, I have given the children of Levi all the tenth in Israel for an inheritance, for their service which they serve, even the service of the tabernacle of the congregation.

skills are not up to par, you will not get the maximum results.

Communicating with your congregation has never been easier. Not communicating is a mysterious and masterful feat. With all of today's technology, there is very little excuse for not getting the word out.

Many times, not-for-profit organizations make the mistake of imparting too much information. They feel obligated to disclose more than is necessary since they are supported by their congregation/members. Be careful of this.

In the next exercise you will access the communication between you, your staff and congregation.

An Exercise in Communicating

How well do you communicate with your parishioners? This exercise is designed to assess your use of current technologies and to give you ideas about ways to communicate with your parishioners. If most of the information you impart to your congregation comes from the pulpit on Sunday morning, you are reaching a very small portion of your congregation.

Profile of Church Communications

1. Do you produce a monthly newsletter? ☐Yes ☐No
    - If you do not have a newsletter, do you have a monthly calendar?
    - Is a calendar of events included? ☐Yes ☐No
    - How is it distributed? _____

2. Do you produce a monthly calendar? ☐Yes ☐No
    - How is it distributed? _____

Getting the Word Out

3. If you do not have a monthly newsletter or calendar, how do your parishioners find out about events?

_____
_____
_____
_____
_____

4. Does your church have a Web site? ☐Yes ☐No

   If yes, answer the following questions:
   - Is your mission statement posted? ☐Yes ☐No
   - Do you accept online donations? ☐Yes ☐No
   - Is your monthly calendar posted? ☐Yes ☐No

   If no, answer the following questions:
   - Why not? _____
   - Do you plan to develop one within the next six months? ☐Yes ☐No
   - Will you accept online contributions? ☐Yes ☐No

5. Do you have an annual meeting? ☐Yes ☐No

   If yes, when is it held?

   How does your congregation find out about the meeting?

   _____
   _____

6. Do you offer the financial details of the church to your congregation on an annual basis? ☐Yes ☐No
In what format is this offered? _____
_____
_____

7. When you ask for money because income is low, do you detail what the money will be used for? ☐Yes ☐No

8. When you need money, are you using Sunday mornings as your platform? ☐Yes ☐No

9. How do you notify your congregation of future events?

    Select all that apply:

    ☐ Announcements

    ☐ Phone Calls

    ☐ Web site

    ☐ Flyers

    ☐ Mailing

10. Are the elders/vestry/deacons elected by the congregation? ☐Yes ☐No

If no, how are they selected? _____

    How long is the term for each? _____

    Are the terms staggered? _____

Getting the Word Out

11. Do you have a rector's warden or pastor liaisons?

    ☐Yes ☐No

    If no, who is available for your congregation to speak with in the absence of the pastor?

    _____

12. Do you have a people's warden or equivalent?

    ☐Yes ☐No

13. Do you hold an annual ministry fair? ☐Yes ☐No

    If yes, when is it held? _____

    How does your congregation find out about it?

    _____

    _____

    If no, how do your parishioners find out about the different ministries?

    _____

    _____

    _____

14. Do you have welcome package for newcomers and visitors? ☐Yes ☐No

    If yes, how do they receive it? _____

    If no, how do you get information to newcomers and visitors?

    _____

15. Is a family profile done each year? ☐Yes ☐No
    If yes, how do you get them to the congregation?
    _____

    How do they get it back to you?
    _____

    If no, how do you keep track of household changes?
    _____
    _____
    _____

16. Do you have an Information Change Form?
    ☐Yes ☐No

17. Is the pastor's anniversary celebrated annually?
    ☐Yes ☐No
    How is it celebrated? _____
    _____
    _____

18. Do you have a pastor's appreciation celebration?
    ☐Yes ☐No

If yes, how is it celebrated? _____

_____

_____

If no, what is done to show the pastor appreciation?

_____

_____

Communications goes both ways!

As much as you need to communicate with your parishioners, you need them to communicate back with you and your staff. It is up to you to make yourself approachable. In doing this, be careful of gossip.

You do not want to hear trivial information, but you do need to be kept abreast of what is going on in town hall. How well this is controlled is up to you. Once you let the gossip in, it stays in, and you get the reputation of being a pastor who loves gossip as opposed to a pastor who holds himself/herself above it.

The congregation should not sit back and expect all the efforts to communicate to come from the church without any input or assistance. It should be just as important for the congregation to speak comfortably to its pastor and church staff as it is for the church staff and pastor to speak with the congregation.

In order to ward off potential problems and possible disasters, everyone should be receptive to hearing what the other has to say. If one half of the congregation feels stifled, true potential will not be reached.

Although you want your congregation to feel that you are approachable regardless of the subject, it will help if you have particular people on your staff that handle certain things. For example, if garbage cans are all over the parking lot because of last night's storm, you would prefer that that information go directly to the facilities caretaker.

Chapter 9
A Sure Negative Response

For the Church

10 Things Not to Do When Asking for Time and/or Money

The following things – although not necessarily wrong – can elicit a negative response from your congregation. If you are currently doing any of the following, take a moment to think about why you do them and try to adapt a more positive spin on the same actions. In this section, we offer alternative actions you can consider.

> **Luke 4:4**
> And Jesus answered him, saying, it is written, that man shall not live by bread alone, but by every Word of God.

1
Be careful how you ask for what you need.
Saying that the church needs new carpeting will probably get you very little assistance; you must know your audience. Perhaps half the congregation present needs new carpets! Why is your need

greater? Make a statement that says that the carpet is presenting a hazard to the church office staff. Explain how it is not in this year's budget to get new carpeting, and then ask for assistance.

If you have been planning carefully, new carpeting would be in your list of items needed over the next five years. Do you have a five-year capital expense plan? If you do not, now is a good time to develop one.

Here is how:

Establish a small committee of two or three people. Have them walk the church grounds and go through the church, the rectory and all other buildings, including all hidden spaces (like under the stairs). During their walk-through they should list everything that appears to need work over the next five years. They should also access office equipment such as copy machines, phone systems and computers.

Next, they should place the items into categories, such as: roof, building interior and exterior, physical building, front grounds, rear grounds, walls, windows, etc.

Remember, this is a plan, and plans can change; so be prepared to shuffle things as sudden needs arise. This will allow you to at least place these expenses into your annual budget or to plan a capital campaign.

2
Having clauses like "we reserve the right to use all donations as we see necessary" can hinder giving.
If I am donating money for church flowers at Easter, I expect my money to be used for church flowers at Easter. If I am led to believe that my donation will be used for any other reason, not only will I become suspicious, but I may also choose not to give it or lessen my donation.

I clearly understand that churches fall upon hard times, but moving donations is not the answer. This business practice can diminish the possibility of future donations. Quite frequently, people leave long-term gifts for a particular purpose and want to trust that their wishes will be fulfilled.

If you are set on using this phrase, be more specific. Perhaps you can state that only offerings beyond tithes fall into this category; or all monies donated that are not earmarked.

Remember, people like giving to specific causes and projects.

3
The more information you hide, the less you get.
Do not be afraid to share financial information with your congregation. You are a not-for-profit organization, and your records should be a matter of public information.

4
Do not sound competitive or demanding when asking for what the church needs.
People have enough areas in their lives where they are pushed around. Compassion and understanding is expected within the church. Present your proposals that way. Remember that many of the people in your congregation may have the same or similar needs in their personal lives. You are asking them in some cases to place their needs second to that of the needs of the church.

> *Do not tell your congregation what you need,*
> *explain to them what your need is.*

5
Do not keep financial secrets; they have a way of getting out.
If your church is having financial difficulties, keeping it a secret will not help. You want your congregation to know that things

are difficult. The secret is in how effective and thorough you are in sharing this information. The information you share does not have to be elaborate. It should be clear and concise; just enough for people to understand and want to help.

6
Do not ask your congregation for input if you have already made the decision.
People will find this insulting and a waste of their time. If you are the decision-maker, make the decision. If you want input, be sure that it is genuine.

7

Be careful when asking for something too specific; at the same time do not be too vague.
If the church office needs new computer equipment, state that; do not say the church office needs new equipment. This will raise questions. "What equipment?" someone will ask. At the same time, don't say, "The church office needs new computers and 17-inch monitors." This is too specific. What if you get a great deal on 19-inch monitors? Someone will remember that you asked for 17-inch monitors, and will remind you of that. Just say the church office needs new computers and monitors.

8
Your personal business it just that... personal!
The more of your personal life you disclose, the more you are placing yourself in conflict with someone else. Of course it is great to share your life as it pertains to the sermon or text; and of course you have close friends within the church that you share your personal news with, but be careful in the pulpit. Telling the congregation that you purchased a new BMW when many of them are struggling to keep their six-year-old car on the road may not serve in your best interests. You do not want your congregation to feel that they are working to buy you a new car or that you are placing yourself in a higher class. If telling your congregation that you purchased a new car is necessary to make a point, then just say that. The make and model may end up being too much information.

9
Do not make people feel guilty.
If your way of increasing giving is to make your parishioners feel guilty for not giving or not giving enough, you should find a new approach. Making someone feel guilty about not giving will not cause that person to write a larger check. For many people, the checkbook will be closed faster! Remember that as human beings everyone has the option of how to spend their money. Your job is to help them see what God has asked us to do.

10
Poorly kept facilities.
Make sure the facilities are kept neat and clean. "Where is my money being spent?" your congregation may ask. Small things like no paper towels in the restrooms can create a negative stirring within your church.

Chapter 10
How to Receive More

For the Church

10 Ways to Assist Your Congregation in Giving More.

By now, you are filled with great ideas on how to inspire your congregation to give more. We would like to give you 10 shortcuts to help your reach your goals.

> **Deuteronomy 14:28**
> At the end of three years thou shalt bring forth all the tithe of thine increase the same year, and shalt lay it up within thy gates.

1
Volunteer Information.
Let your congregation know what is going on before it happens. Being informed makes people feel like they are a part of the group. Hearing things "through the grapevine" is not always best. This leaves room for speculation and fabrication. Be up front and clear. Take ownership of situations.

2
Share the Budget.
In any not-for-profit organization, contributors are always wondering where the money is going. When a grant proposal is developed, one of the key sections includes the income and expense statements along with project budgets. Why should it be any different within the church? Do not be afraid to disclose information about the church finances. If you behave like the finances are a secret, people will wonder what you are hiding. These feelings can cause people to take pause and look at what they are giving and sometimes make an adjustment that is not in the church's favor. Let your congregation know what is coming in and what is going out.

3
Be Available.
Nothing is worse than a pastor who is not accessible. If you have specific times when your parishioners can drop in, let these times be known. I worked in a church office for a while and found that people are constantly just dropping in; perhaps they are just in the neighborhood, or something is on their minds. Whatever the reason, they got to see the pastor. This visit may have disrupted the pastor's schedule, but the payoff is the potential increase in this person's giving next Sunday.

I know a pastor who does not receive visitors when he is working on his sermon. This is a well-known fact within the church. If someone stops by the office during this time, they are informed that the pastor is working on his sermon and are asked to schedule an appointment or leave a message. Unless it's an emergency, the parishioner is fine with this.

4
Develop a Web site.
What a great way to communicate! Your church's Web site can serve several purposes:

- Communication
- Receive donations
- Request information
- Online surveys
- Ministry awareness

If you do not have a Web site, put this at the top of your list of things to do. If you are concerned about cost, you can launch a simple Web site with very little cost. There are several hosting companies available, and they each offer many different solutions. Take the time to shop around. Also, use your resources. There may be someone in your church who can design and maintain the Web site.

5
Make Giving Easy.

Suggest easy ways for your congregation to give. I am a firm believer in being in the presence of the Lord. However, what happens during the summer months when many people take long vacations, or when someone is sick and cannot attend church? How do these people get their tithes/offerings to the church? Today, with online banking, it is easier than ever to send contributions. Help educate your congregation on how to use today's technology. Offer seminars. Help your congregation to understand that giving does not stop because someone cannot make it to church.

Accept online donations!

6
Share the Good Stuff.

Everyone loves good news. If your church receives a grant, share that information. If you recently acquired new equipment for the church office, share this. Let your congregation know where their money is going.

Share the good news of the congregation.

- Who just had a baby?
- Who just graduated from college?
- Who just purchased a new home?

7
Use Bulletin Boards.
Free Press!

> **Deuteronomy 14:29**
> And the Levite, because he hath no part nor inheritance with thee, and the stranger, and the fatherless, and the widow, which are within thy gates, shall come, and shall eat and be satisfied; that the Lord they God may bless thee in all the work of thine hand which thou doest.

If you have a bulletin board, use it! If you do not have one, get one! Post all upcoming events. Flyers are great. They are cheap, quick and easy to create. With today's software packages your office staff can design flyers for your events or create scrapbook pages of previous events. Make sure that all flyers are posted, and keep an ample supply on a table for people to take. If you have a monthly newsletter make sure the flyer is included.

8
Know Who Gives.

If you review the giving patterns of your congregation, you will most likely find that approximately 50% to 80% of your revenue is coming from a small group of parishioners. If these parishioners were to move away, die, or just leave your church, how much would this loss of income affect your income structure? You should consider this. Every church has a group of top givers, and this group should be recognized and made to feel appreciated.

When was the last time you held a dinner or luncheon for the top 10 or 15 contributors within your church? This excludes ministry leaders. Hopefully, you are already doing something for them annually. Do you make sure that this group of parishioners receives a Christmas card? When there is an urgent need and they come to the rescue, do you send them a thank-you note? It is easy to say that they give because they understand their responsibility to God. But realize that they could just as easily give their time, money and talent to another church.

These parishioners are an investment, and like all investments they should be nurtured with care, appreciation and great understanding of their generosity. They should also be acknowledged. You do not need to tell the congregation what and how much these individuals give – that is protected information – but you can let these parishioners know that you recognize them for what they have done and are doing. This is more information for your newsletter.

If you host a dinner for these parishioners, ask them to bring along a guest. Generous people usually have generous friends. Do not ask for anything at this dinner. This is just to say thanks and provide a wonderful evening of food and fellowship. The return on this dinner will be felt during your next fundraiser or stewardship campaign when you ask these people to participate or sit on a committee.

It is very difficult for some people to ask for money. In fact, I recommend that the asking be done by a parishioner some of the time. If your church wants to embark on its first major capital campaign or fundraiser, hiring a professional to help you get started would be well worth the cost. What it would cost to hire someone to organize an event designed to raise money is far less than the return on such an event. These events take time and planning.

> I was once approached to assist with the planning and organizing of an ad journal for a church anniversary – a fun and lucrative project that I have organized several times in the past. I was asked in January and immediately assumed the event was taking place in August or perhaps September. Much to my astonishment, the event was taking place in March! Well, this is barely enough time to plan the event not to mention an ad journal.

> I explained to them that the process of soliciting, designing, typing, printing and binding the book would take a few weeks. In order to produce a moderate-to-excellent ad journal, you need several months from start to finish. Producing a mediocre ad journal would have hurt the church in the long run. Those who did participate could be reluctant to participate again in the future.
>
> Give yourself plenty of time to plan your events.

Does your church have a major anniversary coming up within the next year or so? Start planning *now* for this event.

9
Who are your parishioners?

Do you know the breakdown of your congregation by household? Annually, you should request a family/household profile form be filled out. This form can also double as your Sunday school registration form. One of the best times to do this is in June. The family/household profile will help you to track of your church family's growth. If you want your church to grow, you need more than just a weekly count. You need accountability per household, and you need this annually.

People move, get married; people die and families combine households. Have an accurate accounting of your congregation, and get them into the habit of calling the office with changes or you can use a change form. We have developed such a form for you to use. All new members should receive both forms in their welcome package. When people get married, these forms should be sent to the newlyweds.

Do you know what business people are in? Knowing who to call within your parish can also save money and time.

Family/Household Profile Form

Annual Household Profile

Mailing Address

Phone: _____
Fax: _____
Email: _____
Cell: _____

Name	DOB	Grade	Ministry Sign Up

What skills or talents do you have that may be useful to the church?
_____
_____

What type of business are you in?
_____
_____

Physical address is different from mailing address
_____

Annual Tithe
$ _____

Please return to the church office.
Thank you.

Printed on the back of the family/household profile form should be a list of ministries.

Change of Information Form

Change of Information Form	
Name: _____	Effective Date: _____
New Name: _____	
New Address: _____	
_____	
New Phone: _____	
Cell Phone: _____	Fax: _____
Email: _____	
New Family Member: _____	DOB: _____

10
Encourage Testimonials.

One of the best ways to encourage people is through the testimonials of others. Allow your members to testify. It is comforting to know that someone else is going through the same thing you are going through. Many of us think we are alone in our troubles and hard times. Allow members specifically who were non-tithers to testify on the changes in their life after they began to tithe.

Yours, Mine & God's

Chapter 11
A Word to the Faithful

For the Church

Discern: Give clear thought to what your church means to its congregation today and in the future.

Disclose: Do not hide. Share information, history and plans.

Deliver: To fulfill your promise to yourself, your staff, congregation and God. Make good on your word.

In order to receive you must lead.
In order to lead you must educate.

As your church grows, the development of ways to communicate becomes more important. Take the time to education your staff. Work with your congregation to expand communication throughout your church.

Giving your time, talent and leadership will only benefit your church if your direction is clear.

Work with your congregation to build their faith and understanding about giving. Remember giving comes in the forms of money, time and talent. Respect all three, and receive all three equally.

Participation and leadership go hand-in-hand. The greatest program is nothing without leadership and participation.

For the Congregation... for You!

Discern: As a member of the congregation, think about what you can do for your church.

Disclose: Share your skills and talents with your church.

Deliver: To fulfill your promise to yourself and God. Make good on your promises.

**In order to receive you must give.
When you give you will receive.**

As the church gives information, services, assistance, time and love, it builds faith within us. This faith allows us to mature, to give. What we give is money, time, and talent.

How many church functions have been canceled because of the lack of leadership or participation? Each event, program or ministry within the church requires a leader. If we are all too busy to get involved, many of the programs within our church will disappear. You cannot expect the pastor and church staff to do it all. They need you! They need *us*!

This book has shown you how your time is just as important as your money. The greatest program is nothing without participation.

Too often we are looking for equal reciprocation for what we give. With God and the church it does not work that way. Give what you can. Do not worry about your return. If you have faith, your return will be right on time!

"Do not define yourself based upon 'stuff' – whether purchased or gifted. Define yourself based upon what you give! If you store it up, it breeds maggots, but if you give it away it breeds blessings!"

The Reverend Cedric A. Miller
Living Word Christian Fellowship
Neptune, NJ

Yours: The things belonging to you.

How do you define what is yours? Is it the things you purchased? Is it the things given to you? Are all the things you define as yours material in nature? Is God a part of your list of things? What is yours is gifted to you by God.

Mine: The things belonging to me.

A toddler will define all things wanted and needed as "mine" without regard or the understanding that most of those things belong to another. At that age, they are awarded the privilege of loose usage of the word "mine." As an adult we should know better. What is mine is gifted to me from God.

God's: He to whom all things belong – both yours and mine!

Remember, this book is not for a one-time use. Review it as you mature in your personal wealth and giving to yourself, God and the Church.

Remember that the church includes all that is within; not only its possessions, but the staff and all who partake in its rewards – parishioners and community.

I give this book unto the Lord! Amen

Yours, Mine & God's

A Word to the Faithful

Extravagant Stewards
A Prayer

By The Reverend Cedric A. Miller

Dear Father in heaven,
I give you my heart today,
and I open it to the word,
that through this book,
I shall be changed;
my heart will be changed,
my living patterns will be changed,
my way of thinking will be changed.

My heart will be like yours,
my priorities will be your priorities,
and I will come into a new dimension
of relationship with you,
where I recognize that all I have is yours;
all I will be is up to you.

My life is in your hands,
in Jesus' name. Amen

"If a person gets his attitude toward money straight, it will help straighten out almost every other area in his life."

Billy Graham

(Source of quote unknown)

About the Author:

Michelle Whitaker Winfrey has sat on the vestry, long-range planning strategic committees, hosted several cottage meetings and participated in many different stewardship events, as well as chairing numerous fundraising activities within the church. Michelle's list of church involvement extends beyond these areas to include teaching Sunday school, chairing the annual bazaar, designing ad and program journals, capital campaigns, auctions and organizing the church picnic. These posts have given Michelle an insider's view to the operations of a church, and first hand experience in getting people to give not only their money but their time and talents.

Mark Willis, a friend and fellow vestry member writes the following about Michelle:

> "Beware – an innocent comment at an unsuspecting moment around Michelle Winfrey, and you too may find yourself in some embarrassing task, such as authoring an article on a very personal subject. In my case, it happened to me one Tuesday night on the way to a vestry meeting. On this particular Tuesday, the steeple has just been lifted back to its home on top of our church. I was standing there, admiring an old familiar sight that I had not seen for some time. Michelle joined me as I stared, and remarked, 'It seems bigger than I remember.' Before I know it, I am charged with an essay on being part of a family with long ties to our church."

Michelle has a gifted way of getting unsuspecting people involved. Her belief is that everyone has something to offer.

Michelle holds a Master's degree in not-for-profit administration. For over 18 years, Michelle has managed several not-for-profit organizations, focusing primarily on event planning and fundraising. As a professional fundraiser, giving is a way of life for Michelle. She has witnessed extreme amounts of giving to schools, theatre and dance companies and has always wondered why the level of giving to religious institutions does not compare. This book is her way of helping to break these patterns. She shares with you many of the exercises she has done for herself in order to gain greater control and understanding over her giving practices, finances, talents and skills.

Michelle is the owner of godswarehouse.com, a division of Hobby House Publishing Group, which carries an exclusive line of religious gifts and apparel.

She is also the author of a children's storybook and companion activity and workbook: "It's My Birthday… Finally! A Leap Year Story." She has a line of gifts and apparel called "Born on February 29." These items can be found at www.cafepress.com/Leap_Year. These books were written for her son with God's grace. The book you are holding is written for you and the Church, also with God's grace.

Michelle would love to hear from you. She can be reached at Sales@godswarehouse.com.

Divisions of Hobby House Publishing Group

www.godswarehouse.com

www.cafepress.com/godswarehouse
A great place for religious gifts and apparel

www.cafepress.com/leap_year

www.ingramcontent.com/pod-product-compliance
Lightning Source LLC
Chambersburg PA
CBHW030940090426
42737CB00007B/488